Maurice Sendak's storyboard
(with three revisions to the desert scene at
the end of the sequence)

THE LOVE FOR THREE ORANGES

THE
LOVE FOR
THREE ORANGES

The Glyndebourne Version

FRANK CORSARO

STAGE AND COSTUME DESIGNS

MAURICE SENDAK

FARRAR, STRAUS & GIROUX

NEW YORK

Text copyright © 1984 by Frank Corsaro
Stage and costume designs copyright © 1984 by Maurice Sendak
All rights reserved
Library of Congress catalog card number: 84-47773
Printed in Great Britain by Westerham Press Ltd
First American edition, 1984

CONTENTS

L'Amour des Trois Oranges

GLYNDEBOURNE PRODUCTION, 1982

SUNG IN FRENCH

Conductor	*Bernard Haitink*
Producer	*Frank Corsaro*
Designer	*Maurice Sendak*
Choreographer	*Pauline Grant*
Lighting Designer	*Robert Bryan*
Associate Producer	*Robert Carsen*

CAST

Le Héraut	*Roger Bryson*
Le Roi	*Willard White*
Pantalon	*Peter-Christoph Runge*
Trouffaldino	*Ugo Benelli*
Léandre, the Prime Minister	*John Pringle*
Tchélio, a magician	*Richard Van Allan*
Fata Morgana, a sorceress	*Nelly Morpurgo*
La Princesse Clarice, the King's niece	*Nucci Condò*
Sméraldine	*Fiona Kimm*
Le Prince, the King's son	*Ryland Davies*
Farfarello	*Derek Hammond-Stroud*
La Cuisinière	*Roger Bryson*
Linette	*Yvonne Lea*
Nicolette	*Susan Moore*
Ninette	*Colette Alliot-Lugaz*
Le Maître de Cérémonies	*Hugh Hetherington*

PUBLISHER'S NOTE

As the 1982 Glyndebourne production of *L'Amour des Trois Oranges* by Serge Prokofiev was given in French (sponsored by Cointreau SA), we have retained the French names throughout the book and they follow the cast list and synopsis as in the Glyndebourne programme. A new English translation of *The Love for Three Oranges* was made by Tom Stoppard for the Glyndebourne Touring Opera in October 1983.

To clarify for the reader the extremely complicated plot of this 'opera within an opera', we have made the following distinctions: The Glyndebourne audience is *the audience*, the on-stage audience is *the crowd*, the on-stage opera is *the play*, the troupe members are the *actors*, and their parts are *their characters*.

Wherever possible the drawings throughout the book are shown in their original size. Exceptions occur in the endpapers showing the complete storyboard for the opera, in the drawing on page 3 and in the larger curtains shown on pages 72–73, 76–77, 86–87, 98–99 and 124–125. Details from the storyboard shown throughout the book are in their original size.

For invaluable help in locating the Tiepolo drawings to which Maurice Sendak refers, our thanks are due to James Byam Shaw whose researches were published in *The Drawings of Domenico Tiepolo*, London and Boston, 1962.

The final fracas scene—from the storyboard
(see page 122)

The Théâtre Tiepolo—from the storyboard
(see page 28)

To Begin With . . .

Over ten years ago, having acquired a copy of *The Juniper Tree*, the Maurice Sendak–illustrated edition of Grimms' fairy tales, and admiring its art work inordinately, I ferreted out Maurice Sendak's telephone number and made contact with him:

FRANK: I know you, but do you know anything about me?

MAURICE: Do I know you? Of course I know you!

Thereby laying the cornerstone to our mutual admiration club.

After a brief resumé of shared enthusiasms I zeroed in on my target: Opera and Maurice Sendak.

MAURICE: It's been a dream of mine all my life, but I'm mired in children's books. Who would take a chance on such a person?

Ten years and two productions later, it was apparent that Maurice was anything but mired. Mozart's *The Magic Flute* and Janáček's *The Cunning Little Vixen*, two of the most difficult works in the genre, were now established successes—with sets and costumes by Maurice Sendak. Let me state categorically that I would never have attempted mounting these mastodons without him. For besides Maurice, who is there?

(9)

'The Peep-Show' by Domenico Tiepolo, 1791 — Private collection
(see pages 26–27 and 28)

Since all combinations come in threes (Schubert's Divine Triplets, Christ risen from the sepulchre, and three strikes you're out) we awaited our third collaboration with curious expectancy.

Appositely enough, it came in the guise of an invitation from the prestigious Glyndebourne Festival Opera in England: Serge Prokofiev's *The Love for Three Oranges*, or *L'Amour des Trois Oranges* as it was to be billed. Add to the prestige the fact that this would represent a first time for an American artist and director to grace the groves of Glyndebourne, and the occasion seemed an unduly exciting proposition.

Imagine our horror when we had listened to the opera and read through its libretto. After the heady pleasures of Mozart and Janáček—what were we to make of this farrago of outdated opera clichés? A satire on operatic and literary forms, played in a never-never land of puppet fairy tale creations, it appeared a series of conceits, rather than a unified work of art. At best it had the veneer of the Dada kitsch popular in Prokofiev's time but unlikely to interest our own. The libretto was devoid of the kind of human conflict Maurice and I doted on. Wrapped in a cold if brilliant score, it would last but a night in Russia, where nights are longest. Could two men, under six feet, warm up the tundra?

Our immediate reaction was to turn down the offer—but our collective agents, colleagues and spiritual advisers naturally fainted at that prospect. Give up such a plum? *Mishugas!* Get on with it! Show us what geniuses you are!

Intimidated, we signed contracts and awaited inspiration. A month later, rousing ourselves from our torpor we decided we had finally to face the problems at hand. We first took a hard look at the basic storyline of *The Love for Three Oranges*:

The Prince and single heir to the throne of a faraway country suffers from melancholia. The only cure is through laughter. The King, his father, orders the great clowns and mountebanks of the land to come to the rescue. Evil forces equally contrive to bring about the Prince's downfall. Chief among these villains are

(11)

'Punchinello in the Circus, Swinging on a Rope' by Domenico Tiepolo,
1791—Private collection (see page 21)

Léandre, the wily Prime Minister; the Princesse Clarice, pretender to the throne; Sméraldine, a treacherous servant, and her mistress, Fata Morgana, arch-sorceress. A Festival of Laughter is arranged to aid the Prince but all efforts fail until Fata Morgana herself appears and inadvertently falls to the ground. The Prince's laughter at her predicament arouses Fata's ire. She retaliates by placing a curse on the boy, namely that he will fall in love with three oranges and will not rest until he finds them. The Prince and his trusty friend, Trouffaldino, go in search of the magical citruses. They locate them in a distant palace guarded by a monstrous cook. With a talisman from the sympathetic magician, Tchélio, they find and steal the oranges. On their way back to the palace they discover to their surprise that the fruits are growing in size. In fact so large have the oranges become that they are forced to rest in the nearby desert. Maddened by thirst, they split open the three oranges to reveal three princesses inside dying of their own thirst. Only the third princess remains alive, with whom the Prince falls madly in love. Through Fata Morgana's sorcery the princess is transformed into a rat and Sméraldine substituted in her place. The Prince carries home a counterfeit princess. There, through further magical inter-vention, his true love is restored to him, thus completing his cure.

FRANK: Let's start with what we don't like about it!
MAURICE: I keep seeing those *commedia* drawings in my head. They're so wonderful, and yet so lifeless in this opera.
FRANK: All the cabalistic hocus-pocus in the stage directions—and the never-never land setting that defies being grounded! I simply don't know where we are!
MAURICE: Exactly. I feel like I'm listening to music that is standing in a void!
FRANK: Now, in the never-never lands of your picture books, dogs look like dogs, children like children, and demon creatures ditto. Looking at them you know they all have addresses.
MAURICE: Compliments will get us nowhere! Go on!

*'A Punch and Judy Show on the Quayside' by Domenico Tiepolo,
1791—Private Collection*

FRANK: OK. The opening chorus arguing over the supremacy of tragedy over comedy, etc. It's like exhuming that old chestnut: which came first, the chicken or the egg?

MAURICE: Speaking of chickens, what about the shaggy dog ending? A loud chorus of 'God Save the Prince and the Princess'. And boom—curtain! What kind of a crippled finale is that?

FRANK: Maybe Prokofiev got tired—

MAURICE: Or his wife called him in to dinner!

FRANK: And why do they decide during the prologue to perform *The Love for Three Oranges* instead of something else?

MAURICE: Precisely. Why should that angry mob sit still for the *Oranges* story? Was it an unknown work at the time? A novelty that piqued their curiosity? What?

FRANK: You've read the fairy tale Gozzi based his play on?

MAURICE: *The Love for Three Pomegranates* is a grim, bloody and fabulous bit of medievalism—

FRANK: And Gozzi's version, a clever manicure job!

MAURICE: I wonder why Gozzi didn't render the fable more literally?

FRANK: I believe his target was Goldoni, his Venetian rival, who was making a success of introducing human, even common everyday conflicts on stage. *Oranges* was Gozzi's revenge—a reassertion of theatre as spectacle.

MAURICE: Where's Goldoni in *Oranges*?

FRANK: He's probably Tchélio, the 'fake' or 'ineffectual' magician who doesn't even figure in the original fairy tale.

(15)

Costume studies for members of the chorus

MAURICE: We can go on for ever like this. What's there to like?

FRANK: Well, going back to the opening chorus, I made up a fantasy about it—taking place during the Russian Revolution of Prokofiev's own time! The chorus became bloody Bolsheviks breaking heads over the tragic principle as against the comic.

MAURICE: Let Glyndebourne call in Mel Brooks then!

FRANK: Any fantasies on your part?

MAURICE: Well, the crazy transvestite cook amuses me as an image.

FRANK: Anything else?

MAURICE: The oranges aren't pomegranates, and there's no cream cheese for the prince to stain with his own blood as in the original tale, but oranges on stage might be fun. Although the thought of designing three huge balls that open up like a book, with three princesses inside, is the worst kind of children's theatre imaginable.

FRANK: Well, what could they look like?

MAURICE: Listen, am I sounding too jaded? On the surface this should be perfect material for me but it would be like illustrating a book I didn't want to do!

FRANK: Then let's forget Gozzi cum Prokofiev for a while. Let's look at the original source material—a play within a play, produced in the latter half of the eighteenth century, 1761 to be exact. If we're to ground the piece, we need to start there, or otherwise we must think of it in entirely modern terms.

MAURICE: No sir, I'm not interested in some modern 'abstract' design trailing yards of glitzy mylar and chrome.

FRANK: Frankly, neither am I!

MAURICE: Agreed, but frankly I'm getting paranoid. I can't help feeling that whatever we decide on will only be a monumental effort to bring forth a mouse.

FRANK: The piece is hardly more than an hour and a half long and there's more stuff going on in it than in a full scale opera like *Tannhäuser* which is three times its length.

MAURICE: I wouldn't touch that one either!

FRANK: OK. So we do some private research on that period, and keep up our fantasizing.

(18)

*Moveable giant Punchinello figure, with jointed head, arms and legs,
used on each side of stage*

'Punchinello with the Ostriches', by Domenico Tiepolo, 1791—Oberlin College, Ohio

(see opposite and pages 98–99)

MAURICE: For how long?

FRANK: For another week. Same time. Same place.

MAURICE: Oye!

Indeed, the first breakthrough came at that time. Maurice brought me a book containing the drawings and etchings of Domenico Tiepolo, a contemporary of Gozzi's. This rare find was strewn with remarkable pictures of *commedia* life, not just drawings of the comic prototypes of *commedia* scenarios but sketches of clown families—cohabiting together, in their bath, watching a birth, celebrating a holiday, performing in the circus, etc. The drawings were so suggestive of time and place that they seemed totally relevant to our purpose.

An Italian troupe, then, speaking French, the language to be sung and spoken in the proposed Glyndebourne production. A language sanctioned by the composer himself who was obliged with his then collaborator, Vera Janacopulos, to fashion a French version for the opening performance at the Chicago Lyric Opera

The Ridicules (see opposite and page 45)

Costume study for member of the chorus

in 1921, Russian not being as yet an international language in opera houses.

Certainly there were French *comédie* companies at the time, but Prokofiev retained the Italian names for most of the *commedia* characters, leading us to the assumption that an Italian troupe was performing in a language other than their native one. Troupes of Italian comedians conversant with several languages and dialects were continually travelling abroad in search of new audiences and fresh revenue. Hence our fantasy that this was an Italian company in France became rooted. Given the première of *Oranges* in 1761, conceivably this was still a repertory item in many such companies. In trying to establish an exact date for our presentation, I pushed the calendar up ahead in view of historic events *en route*, and I hit on the year 1789, the year of the French Revolution.

FRANK: What would happen if this Italian troupe of ours would be playing a piece glorifying Royalty to a French audience during their Revolutionary period?

MAURICE: *Mamma mia!* Why should they do such a suicidal thing? Are they crazy?

FRANK: Their audience would stone them, right?

MAURICE: Certainly, since the opera celebrates the aristocracy!

FRANK: Ah, so there's the rub! Let's backtrack a bit. Musically, the opera opens as if the chorus is discovered in mid argument.

MAURICE: But isn't it amongst themselves?

FRANK: What caused the argument in the first place? Couldn't they be reacting to something they're seeing?

MAURICE: How do we do that? There's no overture.

FRANK: Never mind that yet. The important thing is that they've come to see a show—which is not a satisfying experience.

MAURICE: And the choice of *The Love for Three Oranges* is?

FRANK: Interesting you use the word choice! If so, whose choice is it and why is it made?

MAURICE: In the score it is the chorus of 'Ridicules' who announce it—but all that chorus stuff is so vague and ill-defined anyway. Who in hell are the Ridicules?

FRANK: What if the choice is imposed on the actors?

MAURICE: By whom?

FRANK: The climate. The Revolution, I mean. Someone connected with the Revolution. If we go along with grounding the opera in this specific historic time, we must invent someone who represents it.

MAURICE: Wait. I'm seeing something. *The Oranges* could be a sort of agit-prop play, as in our own thirties—

FRANK: —still going on in occupied territories.

MAURICE: I like this idea.

FRANK: You know what this means? We'll have to create an entire sub-text so that *it* determines how each and every moment of the opera develops without changing a single line of the actual text or altering a note of the music.

MAURICE: Frank, are we or are we not being a bit desperate?

FRANK: Maybe, but who cares? If it really works, if it really stimulates us, who cares? We can only find a source for our own impulses. Well, how important is that? We're doing the show, aren't we?

MAURICE: Yes. It will be like doing an entirely other opera.

FRANK: In a way, yes. But the piece requires specific focus before it can really come to life and take off. Maurice—Maurice, this might be it!

MAURICE: Well, I like the feel of it.

FRANK: So do I. But let's live with it for a while, examine the text and music to see how truly viable the concept is.

MAURICE: Tell me. Did you get the idea just now?

FRANK: Well, it was the Revolution—the fantasy, that is, about the Revolution—that stuck in my head. And your showing me the Tiepolo drawings. The whole thing suddenly came together.

MAURICE: Then we must call our company the Théâtre Tiepolo.

By next morning we knew we had found our grounding.

Before work on the opera could begin, it was necessary to create the Revolutionary climate and environment in which the play would function.

(24)

Costume study for member of the chorus

Guided by the Tiepolo drawings, we devised our Théâtre Tiepolo. We placed it under an improvised tent on the quay of a French seaport town, some place like Calais or Bordeaux. The actors would perform on the central platform, and the crowd would assume their places behind the fence and (taking a cue from the score) on a tower alongside it.

(25)

Maurice Sendak's pencil drawing of the Glyndebourne stage at the start of the evening (see page 33)

Next, Maurice drew a series of sketches describing the actors from the troupe at leisure, or between performances. We fashioned our own characters and visualized them as people outside their rôle in *Oranges*.

We created a series of threads between these 'relaxed' images, and decided that before a single note of Prokofiev was heard, we would establish a pantomimed Foreword to the opera's Prologue.

The Glyndebourne stage was adapted for our Foreword. There was to be no curtain. Further, we would take advantage of the side stages peculiar to the Glyndebourne auditorium. They would function as flexible acting areas, initially representing a back-stage view of the Tiepolo troupe, and later as another vantage point for the crowd to view the play from.

We planned that the first three scenes of the opera which follow the Foreword and Prologue would be played on the same setting. Each change would be accomplished by a vista. Maurice devised drops that would descend from the flies, indicating a change of scene. These were placed on opposite sides of the platform, forcing the crowd to move to either side of them in order to get a clear view of the proceedings. This mobility on their part suggested further such variations as the opera continued.

MAURICE: The colour schemes of the sets and costumes are based on the Tiepolo drawings. I'm working to reproduce that delicate, undulating sepia-line and peach grey look of his work. In essence I'm designing a series of huge watercolours. The costumes, in stronger bolder tones, will act as contrasts.

The Foreword and
The Prologue

Two children dressed as cupids
(see page 33)

The Prologue mise en scène

A part of The Prologu

The Foreword

Using the Glyndebourne schedule of operas for the season as our source, we placed an easel on the platform to be seen by both the crowd and the Glyndebourne audience. On the stand were a number of placards bearing the titles of the entire repertoire of the Théâtre Tiepolo: *Orfée, Don Juan, Le Barbier de Séville, Le Chevalier à la Rose* and last, *L'Amour des Trois Oranges*—all historically tenable. The title on top was *La Surprise de l'Amour*—ostensibly the play to be performed that evening. The title is based on a play of the period by Marivaux suggesting frivolity afoot.

This then was the initial image which greeted the members of the Glyndebourne audience as they entered the auditorium—a stage seen 'with its pants down'; actors' laundry on an improvised clothes-line, props and bits of scenery strewn about from the previous night's performance, all bathed in the afternoon sunlight.

As the audience continue to gather in the house proper, the actors begin to filter on stage. The house lights in the auditorium are still up, creating a symbiotic relationship between the audience and the stage.

An actress dressed in Medea-like costume and wig enters. She sits, reading a newspaper. Two children follow, dressed as cupids. They play ball before joining an actor (Roman soldier) in a game of dice. Long pauses are taken between entrances to lend an unhurried tone to the proceedings. A clown on stilts enters next, exchanging juggling pins with another clown. He then crosses over to the right forestage and indulges in a conversation with an actor who later appears as Pantalon. He climbs one of the rope-ladders at the side of the stage to test their stability. Two amorously involved couples follow: the first two start to limber up. Later this pair will portray enemies when they perform in *Oranges*, as will the second couple, the singers who will become the Prince and Fata Morgana.

(33)

At a more accelerated pace, the actors and acrobats come on. They clear the Tiepolo stage, and indulge in quiet conversation with one another. A man in breeches and shirt sleeves bustles about organizing the crew for tonight's performance. This is the general manager of the troupe, who also takes several acting rôles in *Oranges*. Suddenly, the representatives of the Revolution enter: a dark frocked gentleman, wearing a tricolour ribbon, with several attendant officers and soldiers. No one pays much attention to them until several cannon shots are heard off-stage. One of the ships in the background, the one flying the royalist flag, founders, catches fire and sinks in the bay. The entire troupe turns to stare at the Revolutionary official, who, with a slight gesture, signals for them to go on with their business.

Through the smoke of the cannon blasts, the crowd can be seen arriving behind the fence and on the tower. They represent various aspects of the new *bourgeoisie*, carrying picnic baskets and wine bottles.

(34)

By this time the acting platform has been entirely cleared of its odd-ended pieces. The orchestra in the pit now begins to tune up, and the actors retire off-stage to their dressing rooms.

The stage platform remains empty while the last of the crowd trickle in. The house lights are dimmed and the orchestra ceases its commotion. There is an expectant pause, punctuated by the crowd's signs of impatience for the performance to begin: a hint of the chaos to come.

Costume studies for members of the chorus (left and above)

Costume studies for members of the chorus

The Prologue

The Prokofiev Score: The crowd watching the play argue amongst themselves as to the supremacy of tragedy over comedy over romance, etc. The announcement that *The Love for Three Oranges* is to be performed temporarily mollifies them and the presentation begins.

*

The Corsaro/Sendak Version: The lights shift and focus, as a clown appears holding up a frame representing a window. From the opposite side of the stage the actress seen earlier limbering up with her lover makes a theatrical entrance dressed in a Columbine costume. Some members of the crowd begin to grumble, escalating into catcalls as the actress's paramour follows her dressed as a gondolier. The actors seem nonplussed at this unexpected reception. A disgruntled member of the crowd boldly shouts the opening lines of the libretto, 'Donnez-nous la tragédie.' Another voice in opposition counters, 'Non, la comédie.' As the general manager runs on-stage to appease them, the orchestra strikes up the opening measures of the score, which becomes an intensification of the babble on stage.

The Revolutionary faction is forced to interfere as the crowd threatens to get out of hand. The official approaches the general manager, and they stand before the placards bearing the titles of the company's repertoire. Many members of the troupe reappear at the side-stages, drawn from their dressing rooms by the fracas; they are only half costumed. They watch as the manager reveals the names of the works available as substitutes for *La Surprise de l'Amour*. The extended opening chorus of the opera is the background to this action. Each suggestion is turned down, until the final placard reveals *L'Amour des Trois Oranges* which seems to win the consent of the Revolutionary official acting as the arbiter of the arts. The decision is made and the manager holds up the placard for all to see — two bars later a group of the semi-robed actors pick the cue up and reinforce this decision by singing out the name of the chosen play. It is evident that the choice has created a mixed reaction amongst the actors, the reason for which will gradually unfold.

The manager is handed the worn prompt book of the, by now, old play and he begins to intone the opening lines. Bedlam ensues behind him as the actors and stage hands try to find the appropriate props and costumes.

The *Oranges* part of the opera is finally under way.

Costume studies for members of the chorus

An early study for The Prince (not used)

ACT I

Scenes 1, 2 & 3

The court physicians examine The Prince—from the storyboard
(see page 43)

Pantalon, the King's chief jester (left), and Trouffaldino,
a master clown (right)

Act I, Scene 1

The Prince is being examined by court physicians. The only possible cure for his maladies, they declare, is laughter. The King and Pantalon, his chief jester, call upon Trouffaldino, a master clown, to aid the Prince. Léandre, the Prime Minister, is against the idea but the King pursues his plan to cure his son.

*

By now the actors have found the proper wigs and costumes, and they file on to the stage in the dark. The last to enter— a beat late (registered cunningly by the conductor)—is the actor playing the King. He had to change his gondolier costume for royal attire.

MAURICE: The King is called the King of Clubs in the text, but we must avoid dressing him or any of the other characters as playing cards—even though there are several suggestions of that in Prokofiev's directions.

FRANK: Why do you feel that way?

MAURICE: The King is a sad, weary old man desperately worried about his son. It's difficult to act humanly if you're dressed as a card.

FRANK: What about Pantalon?

MAURICE: Well, here is my variation of him, based on the old Tiepolo sketches and wearing the traditional eighteenth-century attire [opposite].

FRANK: Will the same go for Trouffaldino?

MAURICE: Even more so.

FRANK: Incidentally, can his entrance be on one of the ladders?

MAURICE: Very Tiepolo. We'll lower him from the flies.

FRANK: Now what about the Prince?

MAURICE: They just talk about him. He's not seen.

FRANK: I think it's important to see him.

MAURICE: Why?

(43)

FRANK: He's the main character of the opera. He will be invaluable in carrying out that part of our concept dramatizing the tension between the actors and the crowd. We must establish him early on.

MAURICE: All right—so he's on stage. But he's supposed to be sick. How can we involve him in any kind of action?

FRANK: Let's take a look at the chorus' rôle in these scenes first.

MAURICE: Oh, such a mess—I know.

FRANK: Let's say their identity tends to blur out at the edges. Bernard Haitink is a very co-operative conductor. He's agreed which lines can go to the crowd and which belong to the so-called

The sick Prince (left) and the court physicians (above)

Ridicules—our all-purpose chorus in the opera. Making this clear distinction is absolutely essential to the plot.

MAURICE: I thought we weren't going to tamper with the music.

FRANK: We haven't. We've merely reassigned sections to where it helps clarify the concept.

MAURICE: Is that really kosher?

FRANK: The conductor thinks so.

MAURICE: So how does a silent Prince help in this instance?

FRANK: In several of the subsequent scenes, the crowd will interrupt the action with their jibes and comments. The 'characters' on stage will drop their rôles for a while and become the actors again—reacting against these interruptions.

(45)

MAURICE: Do they sing anything which can support this idea?
FRANK: Examine the lines which follow the crowd's heckling of the actors. Notice, the chorus sings, 'Mascarades c'est maigre'. This is intended in the score for the Ridicules. Instead, in the mouths of the crowd, it becomes a taunt. Léandre's line which follows is swallowed up by their interruption. The actors then break their character poses. Léandre next says, 'Cela est bien inutile'. The Prince comes out of his white-faced stupor to glare angrily at the crowd. Pantalon simply says, 'Ah!' in disgust. The King (along with the general manager who has reappeared to get the play going again) rallies the actors. The King says, 'Il faut toujours tenter la chance', then resumes his kingly attitude and continues on 'in character'. This doesn't for one moment conflict

Léandre, the Prime Minister

An early costume study for The Prince

with the actual notes in the score. On the contrary, by emphasizing our point of view, it enlivens it.

MAURICE: Then if the Prince is on stage we must really devise a very special look for him.

FRANK: Way out, but for one thing, make sure you paint his other side so that when he turns to admonish the mob . . .
MAURICE: We see something like this.

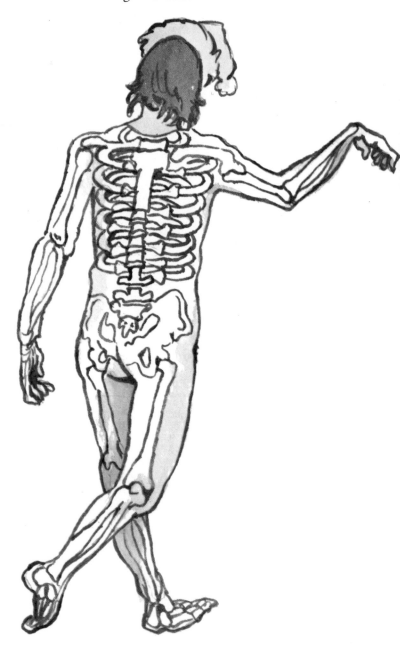

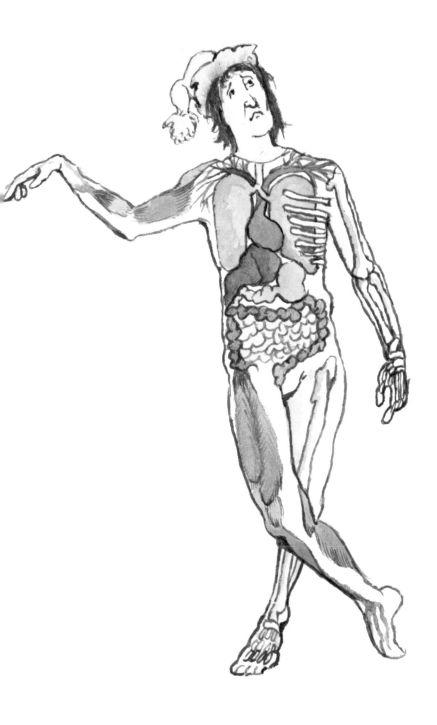

Tchélio, a magician

Act I, Scene 2

Fata Morgana, the evil witch, and Tchélio, the King's sorcerer, vie for supremacy over the Prince's destiny by playing a game of cards. Fata proves the victor and lords it over her opponent.

*

An early sketch for the Fata Morgana screens (see below)

Described in the score as taking place in front of a curtain of cabalistic design. The atmosphere is dark and sombre.

FRANK: This scene does not occur in Gozzi's play. It was Prokofiev's effort to introduce Gozzi's anti-Goldoni character, Tchélio, the ineffectual sorcerer, being bested at a game of cards by the super theatrical witch, Morgana.

MAURICE: Cards again!

FRANK: The direction is that they play before large reproductions of the King of Clubs, and Léandre, who in the list of characters is also supposed to be dressed as a playing card.

MAURICE: I thought we dispensed with that notion!

FRANK: We'll need the cards—the text refers to them—but they will serve secondary purposes.

(51)

Designs for the over-sized playing cards
(see page 58)

Drop screen for Act I, Scene 1

Drop screen for Act I, Scene 2

Drawings for Fata Morgana, a sorceress, and her dog

FRANK: Speaking of satire, this scene is a sort of comic Venusberg, with Fata as a lumpish siren. The alternative is another of those witches who have first dibs on the dry ice concession in opera.

MAURICE: Let's make her sexy, but funny.

FRANK: And ultimately a grotesque who tickles Tchélio's carnality (appealing to his baser instincts—*pace* Goldoni), Fata deters him from playing the proper cards, causing him to lose.

MAURICE: But you said they wouldn't play.

FRANK: They won't. We'll invent a couple of surrogates who will.

MAURICE: What kind of surrogates?

FRANK: The score calls for little devils here. Let's make one of the children Fata's henchman—and for Tchélio—

MAURICE: A commoner—

FRANK: Naturally, Tchélio being Goldoni. But let's give him two muscled bodyguards, surrogates in physical power for his own spiritual bankruptcy.

MAURICE: The cards don't have to be real playing cards.

FRANK: Hell, no! Invent your own.

MAURICE: But what's the setting?

FRANK: It's a series of comic-erotic *tableaux* in a Sendak Venusberg. Need I say more? There's even chase music.

MAURICE: A maze.

FRANK: Two screens, manipulated by clowns, with suggestive drawings on them.

Act I, Scene 3

Léandre and the Princesse Clarice conspire against the Prince. Léandre's method is to feed the boy stale philosophies and arcane verses, thus driving him to madness and death. Clarice prefers violent means: poison or a well-placed bullet. Their plotting is overheard by Sméraldine, supposedly a loyal subject of the King, but in fact Fata Morgana's agent sent to spy on the royal household. Revealing her true identity to the conspirators, Sméraldine joins them in invoking Fata Morgana's spirit.

*

FRANK: Each time I've seen *Oranges* both Sméraldine and Clarice were so sketchily drawn as to be non-characters.

MAURICE: What's so sketchy about a character who talks about killing? That's a mad, wonderful termagant in the raw.

FRANK: By the gleam in your eyes I suspect you have already created her.

MAURICE: Voilà, Miss Annie Oakley of Never-Never Land.

FRANK: I love the hat. It really goes with a first-class pretender to the throne. With a hat like that she deserves to be established on her own turf [see pages 61–3].

MAURICE: I smell another scene change.

FRANK: Another drop opposite Morgana's maze—forcing the crowd to move again to watch the action.

MAURICE: What's Clarice's turf to be then?

FRANK: A man who designed a hat like that asking such a question?

MAURICE: I'm asking.

FRANK: Conceive a landscape worthy of that hat.

MAURICE: Well, that means Watteau or Fragonard, gone to seed.

*Princesse Clarice, the King's niece (right) and a sketch
for her swing (above)*

FRANK: Ah, Cythera by any other name! Only one thing is missing—

MAURICE: A boat!

FRANK: I was going to say a swing!

MAURICE: Naturally, a swing, but I like the idea of a boat, too.

FRANK: Where do we put it? How about some attendants instead. It's easier to push attendants around than it is a boat.

MAURICE: Attendants! Servants! Picnic baskets—all surrounding Clarice in her swing with her pistols on.

FRANK: Maurice, this isn't *The Girl of the Golden West*.

MAURICE: OK. Let her servants hold the pistols, in a fancy box of some sort. But if so, how do we know they're pistols? We can't have Clarice do Mickey Mouse opera stuff by pointing to them whenever she mentions guns.

FRANK: She'll use them at an appropriate moment.

MAURICE: On what? Whom?

FRANK: A little target practice. The servants could be holding decoys.

(60)

Princesse Clarice (above and right)

MAURICE: Why not let her use the guns on the servants? That would make her truly rotten. After all, that's what servants were there for in the eighteenth century.

FRANK: Perversity, thy name is Sendak.

MAURICE: It takes one to know one. For that matter, why not let her take pot shots at the crowd?

Drop screen for Act I, Scene 3

FRANK: That would shatter our overall concept—in fact, bring the action to a grinding halt. Remember, Clarice is being played by an actress trying to please her audience.

MAURICE: Wouldn't this fit in with your idea of the crowd goading the actors?

FRANK: Yes. But it would be too violent a step at this point. We're preparing a very long fuse which must only explode in the finale.

MAURICE: Not even a little threat?

FRANK: Look, right after the crowd starts revoicing its displeasure [page 58 of the score] the actors could stop playing their rôles again and the general manager force them back.

MAURICE: But where's my threat?

FRANK: The general manager can hand Clarice the pistols as a means of resuming the play.

MAURICE: Aha! The crowd misconstrues that action—they see a gun and panic.

FRANK: After all, guns are guns and we are in Revolutionary times. The actors resume their places and the play continues. Now, there's your threat.

MAURICE: Thank you. Next, Sméraldine. It says in the score that she's hiding under a table.

FRANK: On which we can have the picnic baskets.

MAURICE: You talk about clutter! I'll forgo the picnic baskets.

FRANK: What's a *fête champêtre* without a picnic?

MAURICE: The table's OK but I don't want to design grass. Sméraldine needs to be hidden in another way.

FRANK: What does the score say about her?

MAURICE: That she's a servant.

FRANK: Then let her be one of Clarice's servants.

MAURICE: But she's spying.

FRANK: She'll be in disguise. Ah! But then how is she to be discovered by Léandre?

MAURICE: Don't look at me. You're the director. Although an idea has just occurred to me. Why not have Sméraldine try to escape when Clarice starts firing at the servants?

(65)

FRANK: Very logical! Maurice, if I could only design.

MAURICE: I wouldn't be here working with you. So, Léandre grabs the fleeing Sméraldine after the shots are fired and the rest follows as written. Good. Now then.

FRANK: You are, of course, referring to the Big Now.

MAURICE: The Big end of the first act Now!

FRANK: The three villains call on Fata Morgana.

MAURICE: And what is the Big Now? There is no indication in the score that she appears. Still Fata must appear.

FRANK: You read my mind.

MAURICE: It's strange that with his incredibly spooky music, Prokofiev does not have her on stage.

FRANK: Well, having established her as a silly twit in the previous card scene, it would be difficult to have her reappear in some sort of fright wig. Prokofiev, I'm sure, decided to leave it up to the power of his music to stimulate the audience's imagination. Besides, the actress playing Fata would not have sufficient time to change to something appropriately malefic. We could enshroud our villains in smoke — or whatever . . .

MAURICE: Exactly — we must address ourselves to the whatever.

Several feeble ideas came to mind but it was not until late evening, after my thumbing through Maurice's picture book biography — *The Art of Maurice Sendak* — that the notion of Fata literally sprang up from its pages. I telephoned Maurice as he was going to bed.

FRANK: Like they say in that song, I think I've got it.

MAURICE: Quick, before my valium starts to work.

FRANK: A pop up.

MAURICE: Do we dare?

FRANK: A balloon pop up! Something that can grow, just as the music does, reaching its full proportions at the orchestral cut off. A gorgeous, beautiful Fata monster — the epitome of no good.

MAURICE: *Gott in Himmel!* A relative just came to mind who would be a perfect model.

The Fata Morgana balloon (opposite)

The Fata Morgana balloon—from the storyboard
(see page 66)

ACT II

Scenes 1 & 2

The Prince remains unamused—from the storyboard

Drop screen for Act II, Scene 1

Act II, Scene 1

Trouffaldino attempts unsuccessfully to amuse the Prince. Finally, exasperated, Trouffaldino scatters the Prince's medicines and orders that he be forcibly conducted to the Festival of Laughter. The scene as described occurs in the Prince's chamber.

*

FRANK: But we must play this scene literally on the stage apron in front of a drop while the Divertissement setting is being prepared behind it [see pages 72–3].

MAURICE: Isn't that too sharp a break in the convention we've established?

FRANK: Not if we have part of the crowd visible. This is carrying our idea of shifting the crowd's point of view to a dramatic next step. By the time we arrive at the desert scene the crowd will become merely off-stage voices.

MAURICE: I was quite concerned about the desert scene and the crowd's felt presence there. That is the high fantasy point of the opera—and should be free of any reality factors.

FRANK: Couldn't agree with you more. Here, however, we'll use part of the crowd on the forestages, surrounding the rope ladders. The Ridicules will have climbed the ladders and will comment on the action from their perches. Visually this will be a piquant intensification of the *commedia* look.

MAURICE: Should there be any indication that we're in the Prince's chambers?

FRANK: I don't think it's necessary. The only musts are his medicines which can be foam rubber cut-outs on a tray.

MAURICE: Why foam rubber?

Drop curtain for end of Act II, Scene 1

THÉÂTRE
TIÉPOLO

FRANK: So that Trouffaldino can toss them out into the audience. A gentle reminder that they, too, are in the act.

MAURICE: But where will the Prince be? In the score he's in bed. That seems to me a very funny image.

FRANK: I agree. But where will we put the bed—and then how do we get it on and off? In fact, there's no space to get it on or off at all.

MAURICE: No boat. No bed. And I gave up a table and grass. Tsk. Tsk.

FRANK: What are you sketching?

MAURICE: I'm imagining the Prince sitting over the lip of the stage, his feet dangling over the orchestra.

FRANK: That's wonderfully droll.

MAURICE: That faraway look in your eyes indicates that you're not satisfied, however.

FRANK: I'm thinking ahead. I'm thinking of the crowd's comments and the Ridicules' answer concerning Léandre and his Martellian verses.

MAURICE: Martellian verses? I don't even know what Martellian verses are!

FRANK: Whatever they are, they too must appear.

MAURICE: You mean like dancing alphabet soup letters? What are we doing? Early Walt Disney?

FRANK: Quick. Free associate for me. Martellian.

MAURICE: Black.

FRANK: Verses.

MAURICE: Poetry.

FRANK: Poetry.

MAURICE: Book.

FRANK: Book.

MAURICE: Sales.

FRANK: Try that one again. Book.

MAURICE: Sales, large sales.

FRANK: OK. Large, black book. There's your Martellian verses. Draw me one.
Bigger.

MAURICE: But how does the Prince get it? Should he have it on his person at the opening?

FRANK: Where would he ordinarily get it from?

MAURICE: Why, Léandre.

FRANK: OK.

MAURICE: But Léandre is not in the scene.

FRANK and MAURICE: He is now.

MAURICE: Besides, his presence will add a dramatic value!

FRANK: We must see how the Prince is being poisoned. Merely alluding to it is not enough. There are far too many things alluded to in this opera that need practical manifestation. Audiences prefer seeing things than hearing, really. Let Léandre bring on the book—the Ridicules actually use his name, vilifying him as if he were there, 'Léandre Canaille'. His appearance will tighten the conflict between the factions of good and evil, and during the following interval we'll stage a fight between Trouffaldino and Léandre.

MAURICE: How? Their costumes have no weapons.

FRANK: Trouffaldino can use his comedy stick as a sword. That's another *commedia* device. Léandre can produce a weapon at the last minute.

MAURICE: Aha! From the book.

FRANK: Where else?

MAURICE: The sword holds the binding of the book together. Léandre pulls it out, the book falls apart in the Prince's lap. I like it. I buy it.

Instead of the all-purpose opera procession (hobbie horses, strutting courtiers, etc.), we preferred to offer an antic drop curtain in front of which the gathering crowd chatters in anticipated excitement [see pages 76–7].

Curtain for the march between Act II, Scenes 1 and 2 (see page 75)

Fata Morgana cut-out from the end of Act II

Act II, Scene 2

Trouffaldino's Festival of Laughter. The Prince is still in the doldrums until Fata Morgana appears and unwittingly causes him to laugh. Humiliated, Fata pronounces a curse on the Prince, namely that he is to fall in love with three oranges and will not rest until he has found them. Fully recovered, the Prince, accompanied by Trouffaldino, starts out on his journey to find the oranges. The scene takes place on a verandah in the royal palace.

*

FRANK: (Part of a letter to Maurice who is on a business trip to California during this period) . . . With the Divertissement we are midway through the opera and the themes we are developing must come to an appropriate first climax. Here are my main concerns:

(a) That the Revolutionary element be re-emphasized. Possibly an incident occurring during one of the three Divertissements called for in the score. A restatement of this fact is crucial to the opera's finale.

(b) That Fata Morgana's curse be visualized. Prokofiev suggests Fata falls down and her legs are exposed, causing the Prince to laugh. Probably he is seeing a pair of kinky, eighteenth-century knickers or underwear of some sort. We'll decide this point at the rehearsal—the actual pratfall naturally depending on the lady playing Fata. The comic Fata must flee in embarrassment, and be replaced in time by the mystical representation of her. Prokofiev's Janus-headed sorceress must be dealt with as we did earlier in the opera, viz: the balloon. We certainly don't want to repeat that trick. So, do you have another relative to call upon, or else transmogrify the balloon into still another *schreck* image of Fata?

Mise en scène *for Act II, Scene 2 (see pages 20 and 84–85)*

Characters from the Divertissement, Act II, Scene 2
(above and right)

(c) The last moments of this act must combine crowd versus actors versus crowd, with the Revolutionary factors involved somehow.

P.S. Are you still thinking of using the Tiepolo print as a basis for your design of the Divertissement set?

Maurice's response to Frank's letter:

My dear Frank,

But of course our faithful Domenico Tiepolo will provide the inspiration for the Divertissement scene. Has he forsaken us yet? I have an unshakable faith in the people I steal from—a certainty that once having invested our trust in them, they will provide everything—just so long (and here is the crucial hitch) as we are certain that in the final cooking and basting we will transform the basic ingredients of their work into something absolutely our own. It is an odd matter indeed, this almost magical union that occurs between stealer and stealee; it is as though I know what I want but can see it only inside (in this case) a Tiepolo drawing and then I can draw it out and make it quite properly my own.

But to the point: See plate 93 of the Domenico Tiepolo book [page 20]. Isn't that the very blue-print of our Divertissement? The balustrade seems perfect—both grand and simple at the same time—the royal family comfortably separated from the rabble. Note the statuary. Couldn't we have fun and invent a series of grandiose, dotty statues that plainly signal a rather degenerate pleasure garden—the perfect place, in fact, for a mad Divertissement? See the narrow basin filled with water, connected to the balustrade—let's fill it up with ducks, birds and fish—all to kick the bucket during some kind of disaster. Yes? No?

There is a suggestion of gardens behind the figures—I'd like to develop those shapes and introduce topiary figures on either side of the balustrade—huge and cut to bizarre shapes (Fata Morgana à la topiary, possible?)—angled so as to lead the eye quickly to the central action, in fact to our balustrade, and setting the scene for mad revelry. I would like the Divertissement to

suggest the effect of a child's panorama paper toy (very popular in the eighteenth century)—the kind you stretch out in the manner of an accordion and then peep into. (They were usually parks or famous gardens.) The charm lay in the enchanting but intense tunnelling of vision to a central point; my central point (not in the Tiepolo picture) would be a benign landscape that would circle behind the King and his entourage. I imagine a serene seascape—perhaps an island with a pavilion in the distance near the water (almost a continuation of the water in the Prologue) just behind the principals. We could do much with water here. Now, I put this all together in a sketch, and joy and inspiration turned into a stomach cramp. *Gott in Himmel!*—it is all so cluttered. What think you? Too much? Makes a delicious illustration but, I'm afraid, a messy stage design (there always will be this collision in my work!).

So—what must we use? (1) The balustrade (I love it, Frank, so bear with me). (2) The water basin (everything watery is good, I think, and I will add a sly, slightly porno fountain spigoting water into it). (3) The land-seascape behind that is both useful and has the added attraction of balancing and holding together a design full of disparate shapes. So what is making the trouble? Alas and alack, my topiary figures are the enemy. It is the thing too much and you will cry about how I've left no room for getting someone or something on or off stage and you will be right. But so are the topiary figures right? Something must lead us into this noisy scene and the topiary figures could be the perfect image. If properly angled, they would lead the eye up to where we want it. The answer might be to cut them down in size—two *kleine* topiaries in the shape of two rats. As you know, later on the piece is rat infested. Look again at plate 93 [page 20], and see the opera monsters instead of Tiepolo ostriches (though ostriches would be lovely for our desert scene). The libretto calls for 'giants fighting Divertissement'—who can blame the Prince for not laughing, it is all so unfunny. Would you consider changing the giants fighting to two opera divas fighting? And wouldn't it be real fun if our divas are cunningly disguised—one female, one male

(85)

The Divertissement backdrop for Act II, Scene 2

divo, super-star opera stars? They could be delicious take-offs and isn't that in keeping with Prokofiev's original spoofing intention? Speaking of *monstre sacré*! What could be more apropos?

But back to the clutter and my old rankling doubt. You've heard me before but it is a vital issue and needs constant airing. I quite naturally still think in terms of illustration and as an illustration this scene is not cluttered—but we are talking about stage design. I think you will agree that the rather stripped compositions in *The Juniper Tree* and even the seemingly cluttered but rather intense and concentrated composition in *Outside Over There* already suggest a growing awareness of—what?—stage sense? Certainly working with you on *Flute* and *Vixen* has developed this new sense of theatrical composition. I hope so. I worry a good deal (as you know) about the possible dire effects of thirty years' worth of composing for the page on my stage designs. Have I, in fact, been able to bridge the gap between these two disciplines? The *Oranges* divertissement seems a perfect example of my dilemma. There is a typical two-step involved here; first I must illustrate the scene as though for a book and then re-order it for the stage. There is as much good in this as bad, I think—and you have wonderfully supported my budding conviction that I am more and more directly composing for the stage. There is, too, the perfect good of simply being ignorant of the conventions of stage design and hauling into my theatre designs all the vast repertoire of my life as illustrator. But more to the point—was this not the very reason you blessedly needed me in the first place? You wanted a fresh, dumb designer and, God help you, you found one.

Maurice

P.S. For our monsters you may pick two of your favourite operatic *monstres sacrés* and I shall pick my own. Their identities must forever remain our secret.

Frank's answer to Maurice:

I think you're right about the topiary figures and the duck pond is a lovely idea. But, best of all, you provided me with an answer to

(88)

The Prince sets out on his journey (see page 79)

the Revolutionary incident needed. Water, water, water, you ask, and water, indeed, we shall have more of. Your central perspective of the bay up centre suggests we can carry on a battle between two sailing ships. Another royalist fatality will sink into your own delicious waves. *Vive la Révolution!* This incident—complete with falling debris on stage—can replace the fountain Divertissement we find so insipid. Trouffaldino can still sing the designated text, but the battle will prevent the fountain business from being actually performed. How right you are. It is more interesting to have a 'musical' battle between a brace of *monstres sacrés* instead of garden variety horrors. It's a sublime idea!! I've decided that the singer playing the Prince will attack the interfering crowd physically in the final interlude of the scene. And the closing tableau will be the crowd seeking vengeance on the singers playing Pantalon and the King who are left behind after the Prince's exit. The Revolutionary guards are unable to hold the crowd in check, and Pantalon's final lines will have a *double entendre*. 'Quel désastre pour la famille. Quelle catastrophe pour l'état.' The general manager will enter as all the canes and umbrellas are about to strike the heads of the two men. The effect will be stylized. The stage manager will point to maestro Haitink who will bring in the brass coda leading to a blessed and well-timed blackout. Actors versus crowd versus actors. OK? And our secret re the sacred monsters will be kept for ever and ever. I swear. *Ti giuro.* May I develop warts if I renege.

The die is cast! Our scheme—eccentrically our own—will steer us through the rest of the opera. The score, with all of its strange disparities, has now become our own. And why not? Published versions of operatic works usually represent the original production. It is one possible (usually most impossible) version. Unfortunately, such texts, printed during the composer's lifetime, have been looked upon as holy writs rather than representing the problems facing publishers. Books, after all, must be sold while the iron is hot. In that light any addenda and emendations in depth to already published material (no matter how enlightening) can only be regarded as an expensive *folie de grandeur*. Let this, our version be a *folie*. Our *folie*!

ACT III

Scenes 1, 2 & 3

Farfarello, a wind devil,
blows The Prince and Trouffaldino to their next encounter—
from the storyboard (see page 93)

Act III, Scene 1

Tchélio calls upon Farfarello, a wind devil, for information concerning the Prince's whereabouts. Farfarello tells the magician that the Prince and Trouffaldino are on their way towards Créonte's Palace. Tchélio intercepts them in their journey and warns them against the monstrous cook guarding Créonte's keep. He gives Trouffaldino a magic ribbon as a protective talisman against the cook's power.

*

The Prokofiev Score: Scene—a desert.

The Corsaro/Sendak Version: Scene—a desert. (Played on the apron of the stage in front of a drop curtain.)

The Prokofiev Score: Tchélio traces magic circles on the ground to summon Farfarello.

The Corsaro/Sendak Version: Tchélio is discovered atop one of the rope ladders. His owl's hat blinks like a beam through the darkness, as he calls on Farfarello.

The Prokofiev Score: Four pages of summoning music—with no further stage directions.

The Corsaro/Sendak Version: With each *fortissimo* outburst from the orchestra, Tchélio gestures towards a theatre box on the opposite side of his perch. A spotlight hits that area, anticipating Farfarello's entrance. No Farfarello. The spotlight fades. This action is repeated several times to Tchélio's growing consternation. The general manager appears on the stage apron, looking up at Farfarello's box. He indicates for the actor playing Tchélio to continue calling, as the opera cannot proceed until the wind devil appears. Finally, Farfarello clambers into the box. He is adjusting his costume. He obviously missed his cue, and offers signs of apologies to his colleagues. The general manager shakes his head and exits.

(92)

Tchélio, a magician

The Prokofiev Score: *Scherzo*—an orchestral interlude.
The Corsaro/Sendak Version: After Farfarello blows the Prince and Trouffaldino towards their next encounter, the pair scurry up the separate rope ladders during the *Scherzo*. They are swung back and forth, as if being airborne.

Costume study for a kitchen devil

Act III, Scene 2

The Prince and Trouffaldino arrive at Créonte's Palace and are terrorized by the giant cook. While the Prince escapes and hides in a pantry, the cook threatens to eat Trouffaldino for supper. Suddenly, the monster spies the magic ribbon, and being enamoured of such baubles, requests it of Trouffaldino. The Prince enters cautiously carrying the three oranges, and Trouffaldino gives the cook the talisman. Preoccupied with the ribbon the cook does not see the Prince and Trouffaldino escape.

*

The Prokofiev Score: Scene—outside Créonte's Palace. The cook (a male rôle *en travesti*) appears at the kitchen door carrying a large soup ladle.

The Corsaro/Sendak Version: Scene—the kitchen of Créonte's Palace. Following the example of our monster Morgana, we fabricated an enormous pop-up nightmare vision of a creature who is a kitchen in one—with moving parts.

The singer's voice is piped through a speaker hidden in the cook's belly. (The bass originally contracted for the rôle cancelled when he discovered he would be merely a disembodied voice, so the singer playing the stage manager took over this function, very much like his rôle throughout our interpretation.) The cook is surrounded by *petits diables* who help stir the pots and torment the hapless Trouffaldino.

The final escape of Trouffaldino and the Prince, bearing three large oranges, is accomplished by Trouffaldino pinning the magic ribbon between the monster's eyes.

The Prokofiev Score: Orchestral interlude.

The Corsaro/Sendak Version: Three clowns juggle oranges. The oranges keep growing until the clowns can hardly manage to carry them off.

Mise en scène *for Act III, Scene 2*

Drop curtain for Act III, Scene 2

The kitchen in Créonte's Palace—
from the storyboard

Act III, Scene 3

The three oranges are so enormous that the Prince and Trouffaldino are forced to rest. The Prince sleeps but Trouffaldino, maddened with thirst, breaks open two of the oranges and discovers two princesses inside, equally dying of thirst. They expire and Trouffaldino flees in terror. The Prince,

Ninette's transformation—from the storyboard
(see page 111)

upon discovering the dead creatures, requests a passing battery of soldiers to carry them off. Breaking open the final orange, the Prince finds the last of the three maidens, also in dire straits. He saves her life and they fall in love. He dashes off to bring the court to meet his future bride. Fata Morgana and Sméraldine appear and transform the Princess into a rat. Sméraldine pretends to be the Princess, and on the Prince's return demands he stand by his promise to make her his wife. Her contention is supported by the King and his courtiers, and the hapless Prince is forced to lead her back to the castle.

*

Princesse Ninette

Princesse Linette (above)
and Princesse Nicolette (right)

Mise en scène *for Act III, Scene 3*

The Prokofiev Score: Scene — a desert. Evening. The Prince and Trouffaldino appear dragging three enormous oranges behind them.

The Corsaro/Sendak Version: This, the high fantasy point of the opera, is also the scene of our most surreal invention. The desert consists almost entirely of a sphinx, and an inexplicable ship's hull (Maurice had at last one of his wishes), complete with a bleached skeleton crew. How had they got there? Well, once upon a time, when the desert was water . . . The crowd observe the action and comment from their seats 'off-stage' — a logical extension of our shifting point of view technique.

(106)

Our biggest problem was the look and substance of the three enormous oranges.

MAURICE: It's all right their being round when juggled by the clowns—but three, enormous, round oranges that open up? I shudder at the prospect!

FRANK: Well, if they started round, we can't suddenly switch to something other . . .

MAURICE: But what sort of effect are we seeking? Romantic? Comic? Grotesque? This act has the most beautiful music in the opera.

FRANK: A comic, romantic grotesque?

MAURICE: I thought you'd say that. Well then, how much of each? Here—I've drawn three circles. Is one to be comic, and the next . . .

FRANK: What do these circles remind you of?

MAURICE: Oh, *mamma, mamma, mia!* Here we go again!—OK. Port holes!

FRANK: What else?

MAURICE: Pools of light!

FRANK: Try again.

MAURICE: Chocolate covered coins.

FRANK: With gold covered tin foil.

MAURICE: They also look like discs.

FRANK: An interesting thought.

MAURICE: Discs—as oranges? How do we get the girls inside?

FRANK: They would be behind—and we could reflect their shadows on the surfaces.

MAURICE: No tin foil, then? Something transparent?

FRANK: Well, if it's transparent we can't get the ladies on stage. Do they remain three singing silhouettes?

MAURICE: Hoops!

FRANK: What?

MAURICE: Hoops. Like in a circus act. Lions and tigers jump through hoops.

FRANK: Why not three thirsty princesses jumping through hoops?

The ship with its bleached skeleton crew (see page 106)

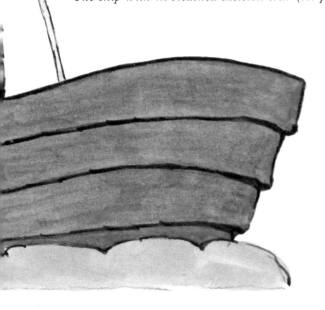

The rat princess (see opposite)

MAURICE: That's certainly comic grotesque. But where's the romance?

FRANK: Everything in this act is done with great *élan*.

The Prokofiev Score: After the Prince awakens to find the dead princesses, and Trouffaldino gone, the score indicates that four soldiers arrive out of nowhere. The Prince asks them to remove the dead bodies, which they do.

The Corsaro/Sendak Version: To keep our story line going, we have Fata Morgana and Sméraldine appear dressed as Bedouins. They are hidden in a sedan chair carried by two strong men. The men place the dead princesses inside the sedan, while Fata watches their rippling muscles with lust burning in her eyes.

The appearance of the third and final Princess, Ninette by name, signals the beginning of an operatic *pas de deux*. Playing to unexpected strength, the singer acting Ninette (Colette Alliot-Lugaz) was a former ballerina, and our Prince (Ryland Davies), enamoured by the idea of turning into an instant singing Nureyev, participated in an unusual love scene—a romantic, comic, lightly grotesque take-off of *The Sleeping Beauty*.

The Prokofiev Score: After the Prince's exit, night falls and Sméraldine appears. Behind her, Fata Morgana is seen in silhouette. Sméraldine carries a huge needle with which she stabs Ninette, transforming her into a rat. Fata suddenly enters and commands Sméraldine to take Ninette's place and await the return of the Prince.

The Corsaro/Sendak Version: Sméraldine and Fata emerge out of the shadows. Still disguised as a Bedouin, Sméraldine approaches carrying a huge hat pin. Under her burnous she is dressed identically like Ninette. The head on the hat pin glows hypnotically. Ninette retreats behind the hulk of the ship. We see Sméraldine raise the hat pin at Fata's command and plunge it into Ninette who screams (out of sight). Ninette is instantly transformed into a huge rat and dashes out into the desert. The horrified sphinx raises its paws in fear as the rodent scurries past it. The royal entourage arrives, and the Prince is forced to take the false Princess, Sméraldine (in disguise), back to the Palace.

(III)

A cut-out desert camel, Act III, Scene 3

As Léandre and Clarice, part of the entourage, gloat over their incipient victory, the skeleton crew raise their arms in admonition and disgust for the dastardly conspirators.

ACT IV

Scenes 1 & 2

The Ridicules flatter Fata Morgana—from the storyboard
(see page 115)

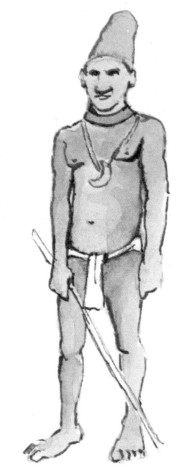

One of Fata Morgana's strong men
(see opposite)

Act IV, Scene 1

Tchélio and Fata Morgana vilify one another, heaping scorn on the cheap magical tricks each has resorted to for and against the Prince. The Ridicules subsequently flatter and manipulate Fata so that Tchélio can have his advantage in helping the Prince.

*

The Prokofiev Score: The scene takes place in front of a cabalistic drop, similar to Act I, Scene 2 (Fata's domain). Tchélio and Fata arrive from separate sides of the stage and begin their argument. Their fulminations are punctuated with thunder claps. The Ridicules sneak onto the stage and humour Fata, with malign intent. They shove her into one of the Palace turrets and lock the door. Smoke emanates from behind it. Tchélio aims a deadly incantation towards the door, and exits with the Ridicules.

The Corsaro/Sendak Version: The scene takes place before the drop curtain on the stage apron.

The two screens seen in the first Tchélio/Fata confrontation reappear and separate. Tchélio and Fata are revealed. As the two sorcerers argue, the Ridicules move the screens to the extreme right and left of the apron. The Ridicules whisper in Fata's ear. They gesture toward the screens which move once more. A near-naked strong man stands on each side of the stage. Fata faints at the prospects standing before her. While she is in a swoon the Ridicules prompt Tchélio to get on with helping the Prince. Fata awakens and escorts her two prize strong men off stage. She gestures tauntingly at Tchélio, who threatens feebly: 'Vois, sorcière, quelle est ma puissance' (and there is another thunder clap). The Ridicules (pointing to the strong men with their comic sticks) answer, 'Tiens, tiens, puissance'. Tchélio makes a haughty and dignified exit.

Ninette occupying the royal throne—from the storyboard
(see opposite)

The rat on the cheese throne (see page 119)

Act IV, Scene 2

The royal entourage returns to the Palace to discover the huge rat (Ninette) occupying the royal throne. Tchélio gestures and the rat is transformed back into Ninette. The Prince claims his rightful bride and the King turns on Clarice, Sméraldine and Léandre to punish them. The villains attempt to escape but Fata breaks through the doors of her prison, and gathering her minions around her, disappears through a trap door. The chorus sings 'God Save the King, the Prince and the Princess.'

*

In essence, this describes the action of the opera's final scene as printed in the score. The following is the outline of our version at Glyndebourne which brought together our various themes. The scene is, as per the score, a Throne Room. We return to our first set, with the crowd in their original place behind the fence. Thus, from a thematic point of view we have made a full circle.

The royal entourage returns to the Palace and discovers a huge rat occupying a Swiss cheese throne.

While Tchélio gestures futilely (Gozzi's satire on Goldoni carried to its extreme), Sméraldine, wielding her magic hat pin, stabs the rat out of pique, unwittingly reversing the magic, and Ninette is restored to her former self.

The King turns on Sméraldine, Clarice and Léandre to mete out their punishment—death, by hanging. The crowd's sympathies have been enlisted by the three anti-royalist villains. The crowd's mutterings punctuate the King's decree. Suddenly Léandre attempts to escape. He brandishes his sword and cuts a swathe through the courtiers. Clarice produces her pistol and shoots down anyone threatening Léandre. One of her bullets blows out the owl lamp on Tchélio's hat, and the magician flees in panic. Sméraldine finds herself faced with a furious Ninette holding the rat pin. Attempting to escape, Sméraldine is stabbed by the Princess and is herself transformed into a rat.

Before Sméraldine can retaliate in kind, Ninette breaks the hat pin in two and tosses the pieces away. The Prince now enters the fray, demonstrating unforeseen prowess with his rapier. He engages Léandre as Fata Morgana arrives through the crowd to dominate the scene.

Fata is depicted as a sort of Madame La Farge. She has been transformed into a veritable symbol of the Revolution—her ultimate bit of magic. She carries a miniature guillotine in the form of a lyre. She calls the villains to her side and they exit in a Delacroix vision of the Revolutionary tomorrow, as Fata strums the *Marseillaise*.

The rat, Sméraldine, dives in and paddles after them. 'Vive la Révolution in Excelsis Gloria Mundi.' The Revolutionary leader and soldiers snigger with satisfaction. 'Vive la Culture Nouvelle.' The actors left timorously on stage intone the final shaggy dog ending. 'Vive le Roi . . . Le Prince et la Princesse.' The crowd mockingly echo the royal cliché accompanied by a

Fata Morgana (see above)

Studies for the King

thumbs-down gesture. After the final musical cut off, the crowd start pelting the actors with oranges, bananas, bottles, etc. (all foam rubber), as the general manager sinks dejectedly on the platform, and the performance comes to an end. It is obvious why the choice of *The Love for Three Oranges* was made in the first place. A Revolutionary piece of propaganda has had its day. The curtain descends over this mêlée as the orchestra repeats the famous march of Act II.

A tableau ensues showing the fracas which has developed between the crowd and the incensed actors.

The stage is littered with rubbish, through which a formal, gracious curtain call is taken by the company in true eighteenth-century style.

FRANK: Well Maurice, what do you think?

MAURICE: *Mamma mia* and *Gott in Himmel!* I can't believe it's the same piece we almost abandoned. I love it.

FRANK: So do I. I don't know whether I love it for what we've done with it or for realizing what the work really contains.

MAURICE: Well, it's as if we've been playing charades.

FRANK: In fact, just what Prokofiev called it. I think he'd approve.

MAURICE: I think he'd approve, too.

FRANK: What's wrong?

MAURICE: Suppose the theatre audience starts pelting us when we take our curtain call?

FRANK: Well, we'll pelt them right back.

MAURICE: *Vive l'imagination et le courage!*

FRANK and MAURICE: *Vive le théâtre!*

The Prince (right) and Sméraldine in royal disguise (left)

The Finale drop curtain

DIRECTOR AND DESIGNER

Frank Corsaro is a man of many parts, a director of theatre and television as well as of opera, an actor, a playwright and an adaptor. His theatre direction includes *A Hatful of Rain*, *The Night of the Iguana*, *Cold Storage* and *Whoppee!* on Broadway, and his many opera credits include *La Bohème*, *Don Giovanni*, *La Fanciulla del West*, *A Village Romeo and Juliet*, *The Magic Flute* and *The Cunning Little Vixen* produced in the United States and Europe. *L'Amour des Trois Oranges* was his first opera produced in England but certainly not his last. As an actor he appeared on Broadway with Helen Hayes in *Mrs McThing* and his screen debut was in Paul Newman's film, *Rachel, Rachel*.

Frank Corsaro is a native New Yorker and a graduate of Drama School at Yale University. He is married to film actress/mezzo contralto Mary Cross Lueders and they have a son, Andrew.

Maurice Sendak was commissioned in 1979 by the Houston Opera in Texas to do the costumes and sets for Mozart's *The Magic Flute*. Already renowned the world over for his outstanding children's picture books *Where the Wild Things Are* and *In the Night Kitchen* (the trilogy completed in 1981 with *Outside Over There*), when Maurice Sendak entered the new field of opera it was to be greeted with rapturous acclaim, and *The Magic Flute* was soon followed by *Where the Wild Things Are* in Brussels, *The Cunning Little Vixen* in New York, *The Love for Three Oranges* at Glyndebourne and a new production of *Where the Wild Things Are* in London.

Maurice Sendak was born in Brooklyn, New York, where he spent his childhood. He attended the Art Students' League for two years of night classes — his only formal art training — and *Kenny's Window*, the first book he both wrote and illustrated, was published in 1956.